W9-CLV-069

? COMMUNITY · CONNECTIONS

WHAT'S IT LIKE TO LIVE HERE?
FARM
BY KATIE MARSICO

Published in the United States of America by Cherry Lake Publishing
Ann Arbor, Michigan
www.cherrylakepublishing.com

Content Adviser: James Wolfinger, PhD, Associate Professor of History,
DePaul University, Chicago, Illinois
Reading Adviser: Marla Conn, ReadAbility, Inc.

Photo Credits: Cover and page 1, ©Sofarina79/Shutterstock, Inc.; page 5, ©Johannes
Eder/Shutterstock, Inc.; page 7, ©Sandra Cunningham/Shutterstock, Inc.; page 9,
©Christopher Elwell/Shutterstock, Inc.; page 11, ©michaeljung/Shutterstock, Inc.; page 13,
©IrinaK/Shutterstock, Inc.; page 15, ©defotoberg/Shutterstock, Inc.; page 17, ©Catalin
Petolea/Shutterstock, Inc.; page 19, ©ER_09/Shutterstock, Inc.; page 21, ©Jaren Jai
Wicklund/Shutterstock, Inc.

LIBRARY OF CONGRESS CATALOGING-IN-PUBLICATION DATA
Marsico, Katie, 1980– What's It Like to Live Here?:
  Farm / by Katie Marsico.
      pages cm. — (Community connections)
  Includes bibliographical references and index.
  ISBN 978-1-62431-569-5 (lib. bdg.) — ISBN 978-1-62431-593-0 (ebook) —
ISBN 978-1-62431-585-5 (pbk.) — ISBN 978-1-62431-577-0 (pdf)
  1. Farm life—Juvenile literature. I. Title
  HT421.M395 2014
  306.3'49—dc23   2013025645

Cherry Lake Publishing would like to acknowledge the
work of The Partnership for 21st Century Skills. Please
visit www.p21.org for more information.

Printed in the United States of America
Corporate Graphics Inc.
January 2014

FARM

CONTENTS

WHAT'S IT LIKE TO LIVE HERE?

COCK-A-DOODLE-DOO!

Kim woke up to the sound of a rooster crowing. Her dad's tractor buzzed in the distance. Kim never needed an alarm clock to wake up. Instead, she relied on the lively morning sounds outside her window. This was one of the best things about living on a farm.

A rooster's crow is one of many sounds you might hear on a farm.

How many farms are there in the United States and Canada? Take a guess. If you said more than two million, you are right!

5

A farm is a piece of land. It includes buildings used to grow **crops** or raise animals. Some farmers **harvest** plants. They might grow corn, wheat, or cotton. Other farmers raise animals. Cows, pigs, sheep, chickens, and horses are common farm animals.

Farms often include large amounts of land that have both buildings and fields.

Think about what other plants and animals are found on farms. Rice, fruit, turkeys, and goats are just a few examples.

Farms are an important part of every **community**. People use farm **products** for everything from food to clothing. Think about what life would be like without farms. Your milk comes from cows on dairy farms. Bread is made from wheat crops. Even the cotton in your favorite pajamas comes from farms!

Milk, cheese, and other dairy products come from dairy farms.

LOOK!

Take a close look around your home or school. What products do you see that came from a farm?

FARM LIFE

Kim had to wake up early for school. She had a long bus ride. Kids for miles around went to that school. Still, the school was small compared to city schools were Kim's cousins went. This is because Kim lived in a **rural** area. Fewer people live there than in the city.

Kim's classmates came from all across the area.

How do farm kids get to school? Many travel in a bus or a car. Some farm kids are homeschooled. This means that their parents or other adults teach them lessons at home.

After school, Kim had to do her chores. So did most of her friends. They helped clean dishes and take out the trash. But they also had other **responsibilities**. These other chores depended on what kind of farm their family owned.

Once the white tufts of cotton burst from their pods, the cotton is ready to harvest, or gather.

Ask adults on a farm what their workday is like. How many hours do they spend caring for the farm? Do they have other jobs as well? How often do they leave the farm? Many farmers work from sunrise to sunset!

13

Kim lived on a farm where **livestock** are raised. Livestock are animals. Kim helped feed the animals. She also helped keep their stables and pens clean. Kim's friend Julie lived on a farm that grew plants. She helped her family plant and gather crops each year.

One of Kim's chores was to feed the family's horses.

Many farmers share close ties. Neighbors often help each other out. Sometimes they fix broken fences. They also lend a hand when natural disasters such as floods hit. Then they help save each other's crops and animals. Why might this be important?

15

EXCITING EXPERIENCES

Kim's cousins told her stories about museums and fancy restaurants. But she did things her cousins never experienced. Her favorite was taking a ride on the family tractor. She also lived far from city lights. This allowed her to see a lot more stars in the night sky.

Tractors are a useful tool on many farms.

Go online or visit
the library. Look
up different types
of farm machinery.
Do they look heavy
or dangerous? It
is important that
farm kids listen to
grown-ups. Everyone
must stay safe while
doing chores and
having fun.

17

Kim's backyard was always busy. There were chickens, horses, cats, dogs, and cows. Her friend Jonathan even raised rabbits. Kim watched chicks hatch from eggs. Tiny seeds grew into tall grasses and bright fruits and vegetables. She worked in barns housing animals, hay, and tools. Tall buildings called **silos** towered above friends' homes.

Some farm kids get to pick strawberries in their own backyard!

Ask a farmer what kinds of animals he or she has. Some farm kids have the same pets as other kids. They might have fish, cats, and dogs. Others also raise animals ranging from rabbits to llamas!

BUSY DAYS

Kim enjoyed her free time in the evenings. Sometimes she visited friends and played games. In the fall, she played baseball on a local kid's team. Kim had a full day. There was always a lot going on around a farm!

A farm is full of all kinds of life.

What kind of farm would you like to have? Imagine living there with your family. Draw a picture of how life on the farm might look.

GLOSSARY

community (kuh-MYOO-nut-ee) a place and the people who live in it

crops (KRAHPS) plants used for food or other products

harvest (HAR-vuhst) to gather crops that are ripe

livestock (LIVE-stahk) animals that are kept or raised on a farm or ranch

products (PRAH-duhkts) things that are manufactured or made by a natural process

responsibilities (ri-span-suh-BIL-uh-teez) duties or jobs

rural (ROOR-uhl) having to do with the countryside or farming

silos (SYE-lohz) tall, round towers used to store food for farm animals

FIND OUT MORE

BOOKS

Cordier, Severine, and Cynthia Lacroix. *A Day at the Farm.* Berkeley, CA: Owlkids Books, 2013.

Flatt, Lizann. *Life in a Farming Community.* New York: Crabtree Publishing, 2009.

Krusinski, Anna. *Farm Friends: A Visit to the Local Farm.* Hobart, NY: Hatherleigh Press, 2013.

WEB SITES

Ontario Agri-Food Education—Farms, Food and Fun
http://www.farmsfoodfun.com/default.aspx
Find out more about what it is like to live and work on a farm.

Kenyon College—Growing Up on a Family Farm
www2.kenyon.edu/projects/famfarm/life/kids.htm
Check out this site to learn more about what day-to-day life is like for farm kids.

INDEX

ABOUT THE AUTHOR

Katie Marsico is the author of more than 100 children's books. She lives in a suburb of Chicago, Illinois, with her husband and children.

24